No.1 for exam success

SATs Skills

Spelling and Vocabulary Workbook

10–11 years

Do not write in this book

OXFORD
UNIVERSITY PRESS

OXFORD
UNIVERSITY PRESS

Great Clarendon Street, Oxford, OX2 6DP, United Kingdom

Oxford University Press is a department of the University of Oxford.
It furthers the University's objective of excellence in research, scholarship,
and education by publishing worldwide. Oxford is a registered trade mark
of Oxford University Press in the UK and in certain other countries

British Library Cataloguing in Publication Data
Data available

978-0-19-274654-2

10 9 8 7 6 5 4 3 2 1

Paper used in the production of this book is a natural, recyclable product
made from wood grown in sustainable forests. The manufacturing process
conforms to the environmental regulations of the country of origin.

Printed in the United Kingdom

Acknowledgements

Cover illustrations: Lo Cole

Although we have made every effort to trace and contact all copyright
holders before publication this has not been possible in all cases.
If notified, the publisher will rectify any errors or omissions at the
earliest opportunity.

Links to third party websites are provided by Oxford in good faith and for
information only. Oxford disclaims any responsibility for the materials
contained in any third party website referenced in this work.

Ⓐ Draw a line to match word to its definition. [16]

1	twirl	Braided hair or thread
2	bridal	Fantastic
3	plaits	My mother's or father's brother
4	blank	A place of worship
5	grateful	To twist or spin
6	laundry	To do with a wedding
7	powerful	Community or communal
8	social	A material
9	wonderful	A missing space
10	selfish	Appreciative
11	claim	Fashion
12	plastic	Washing
13	uncle	Strong
14	style	To drag, pull or heave
15	temple	Not generous or thoughtful
16	lug	To make a statement

Ⓑ Which of your words have these smaller words hidden in them? [8]

1	last _____	**5**	owe _____
2	ate _____	**6**	elf _____
3	dry _____	**7**	aim _____
4	rid _____	**8**	an _____

Ⓒ A synonym is a word that is similar in meaning to another. Which of your words are synonyms for these words? [6]

1	revolve _____	**4**	indebted _____
2	marvellous _____	**5**	authorative _____
3	empty _____	**6**	allege _____

blank

bridal

claim

grateful

laundry

lug

plaits

plastic

powerful

selfish

social

style

temple

twirl

uncle

wonderful

30

alien

auntie

brilliant

carried

cushion

especially

fields

grief

interview

ion

nuisance

period

relief

riot

superior

view

29

(D) All of your words fit into the grid. Work out which number represents each letter to solve the puzzle. [19]

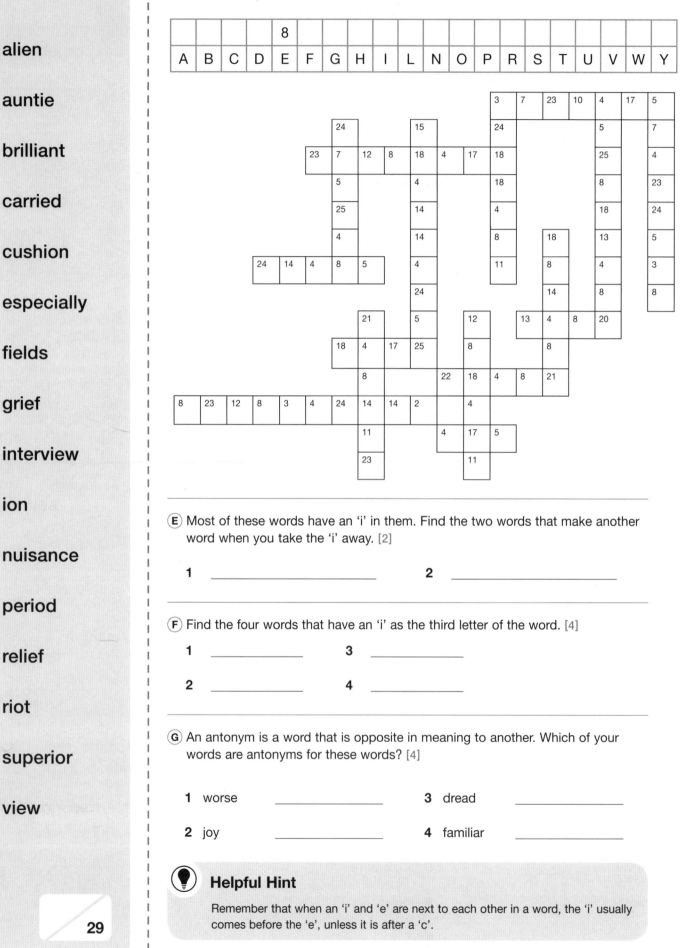

| A | B | C | D | E | F | G | H | I | L | N | O | P | R | S | T | U | V | W | Y |

(E) Most of these words have an 'i' in them. Find the two words that make another word when you take the 'i' away. [2]

1 _____   2 _____

(F) Find the four words that have an 'i' as the third letter of the word. [4]

1 _____   3 _____

2 _____   4 _____

(G) An antonym is a word that is opposite in meaning to another. Which of your words are antonyms for these words? [4]

1 worse _____   3 dread _____

2 joy _____   4 familiar _____

Helpful Hint

Remember that when an 'i' and 'e' are next to each other in a word, the 'i' usually comes before the 'e', unless it is after a 'c'.

(H) Fill in the grid with all of your words, using the clues to help you. [16]

Across

2   A question
4   To stand in a line
7   Not gas or solid
8   To paste or stick
11 Petrol
12 A woodland animal
14 Cookies
15 A road or walkway

Down

1   Mean
3   A dark mark on hurt skin
5   An imaginary line around the world
6   Shape with four equal sides
9   Worth something
10 Succeeds
11 Flows easily
13 To save

(I) Turn the following words into the present participle. [6]

Example: glue _gluing_

1   achieve _____

2   rescue _____

3   bruise _____

4   squirrel _____

5   query _____

6   queue _____

achieves

avenue

biscuits

bruise

cruel

equator

fluid

fuel

glue

liquid

query

queue

rescue

square

squirrel

valuable

💡 **Helpful Hint**

Some of these words can be tricky to spell because of the unusual double vowels. Creating a mnemonic or rhyme to help you remember any that seem especially difficult can be useful.

22

5

Unit 1

alter

corner

crater

customer

danger

disaster

helicopter

hover

lobster

number

partner

prefer

quiver

register

splinter

together

30

(J) An anagram is a word that has had its letters rearranged. Which of your words have become the following anagrams? [16]

1	treal	_____	9	orvhe	_____
2	reviqu	_____	10	pernart	_____
3	ronrec	_____	11	comerust	_____
4	creatr	_____	12	thegetro	_____
5	grande	_____	13	printles	_____
6	merbun	_____	14	thepolicer	_____
7	preefr	_____	15	greetsir	_____
8	bolster	_____	16	stairsed	_____

(K) Which of your words fit these definitions? [8]

1 Hazard _____

2 A tiny sliver of wood _____

3 A client _____

4 To have a favourite option _____

5 To change _____

6 Catastrophe _____

7 Jointly _____

8 Shudder _____

(L) Some of these words can have one letter added to make a new word. Write the new word below. [2]

1 alter + f = _____   2 customer + s = _____

(M) Remove one letter from each of the following words to make a new word. [4]

1 hover _____   3 crater _____

2 danger _____   4 prefer _____

💡 **Helpful Hint**

All of these words end in 'er'. Although some words do end in 're' and 'ar', it is more common for a word to end in 'er'. So if you hear the 'r' sound and you are unsure of the spelling, it is always worth trying 'er' first.

(↻) Recap

(A) All of your words are hidden in the word search. They go across and down, but not diagonally. Find your words and then find the leftover letters. What do the leftover letters spell out? [17]

D	E	S	C	R	I	P	T	I	O	N	S
E	A	T	T	R	A	C	T	I	O	N	E
C	O	N	V	E	R	S	A	T	I	O	N
O	P	R	O	T	E	C	T	I	O	N	S
R	E	C	E	P	T	I	O	N	E	N	A
A	R	D	I	R	E	C	T	I	O	N	T
T	A	T	T	E	N	T	I	O	N	D	I
I	T	I	N	V	E	N	T	I	O	N	O
O	I	N	F	O	R	M	A	T	I	O	N
N	O	W	C	O	M	M	O	T	I	O	N
I	N	S	T	R	U	C	T	I	O	N	I
T	C	O	M	P	E	T	I	T	I	O	N
H	T	I	S	E	C	T	I	O	N	O	N

(B) What is the root word of each of the following words? [12]

1   conversation _____   7   operation _____

2   decoration _____   8   protection _____

3   description _____   9   attention _____

4   direction _____   10 attraction _____

5   invention _____   11 information _____

6   competition _____   12 instruction _____

Word list (Unit 2):

attention

attraction

commotion

competition

conversation

decoration

description

direction

information

instruction

invention

operation

protection

reception

section

sensation

 Helpful Hint

When a word ends in 'e', remove the 'e' before adding the 'tion' ending.

29

Unit 2

bothered

climbed

covered

dodged

encrusted

entered

finished

frowned

haunted

lined

murdered

produced

returned

striped

tortured

wandered

32

(C) Fill in the grid with all of your words. The first letter of each word has been given to help you. [16]

(D) Which of your words have these smaller words hidden in them? You may need to use some of your words more than once. [16]

1	own	_____	9	the	_____
2	bed	_____	10	turn	_____
3	and	_____	11	do	_____
4	her	_____	12	rust	_____
5	she	_____	13	to	_____
6	rip	_____	14	rod	_____
7	urn	_____	15	aunt	_____
8	over	_____	16	row	_____

 Helpful Hint

Most of the time, if a word ends in 'e', to show the past tense we just add 'd' but for words ending in any other letters, we add 'ed'.

8

Unit 2

E) All of your words fit into the grid. Work out which number represents each letter to solve the puzzle. [19]

										6					
A	B	C	D	E	G	I	J	K	L	M	N	O	P	R	S	T	U	V	X

(code-breaker crossword grid)

F) Which of your words fit these definitions? [12]

1 Used to see the night sky _____

2 A break _____

3 A small flow of liquid _____

4 A family member _____

5 Can be seen _____

6 A gentle bend _____

7 To make something seem more than it is _____

8 Used to speak _____

9 To make someone laugh _____

10 To give someone a place to stay _____

11 Disgusting _____

12 Capacity _____

accommodate

curve

exaggerate

joke

negative

pause

positive

relative

repulsive

savage

telescope

translate

trickle

visible

voice

volume

31

almond

answered

arid

crowd

descend

hatred

hind

humid

overjoyed

poked

record

reward

timid

visited

wand

wondered

31

G All of your words are hidden in the word search. They go across and down, but not diagonally. Find your words and then find the leftover letters. What do the leftover letters spell out? [17]

_____

D	E	S	C	E	N	D	A	T	O	H
A	R	H	I	N	D	H	N	V	V	E
R	E	W	A	R	D	A	S	I	E	H
I	C	A	L	E	N	T	W	S	R	U
D	O	N	M	P	D	R	E	I	J	M
L	R	D	O	O	E	E	R	T	O	I
T	D	T	N	K	E	D	E	E	Y	D
W	O	N	D	E	R	E	D	D	E	R
C	R	O	W	D	T	I	M	I	D	D

H Which of your words fit these definitions? [14]

1 Thought _____

2 Back _____

3 Magic stick _____

4 Very dry _____

5 A sweet nut _____

6 Replied _____

7 A large group _____

8 Extremely happy _____

9 Shy _____

10 Prodded _____

11 Loathing _____

12 Drop down _____

13 A prize _____

14 Write down _____

Unit 3

Ⓐ Place one of your words in each space so that the sentences make sense. [16]

1   The wind blew _____, causing little effect to the leaves on the trees.

2   I have a _____ certificate showing the wedding of my great grandparents.

3   There was only one _____ travelling on the bus.

4   We baked a _____ cake for tea.

5   It was _____ of Zara to share her sweets with everyone.

6   I placed the butter in the _____ to keep it cool.

7   There were five birds perched on the window _____ .

8   The white paper is perfect for _____ or everyday printing.

9   It was a real _____ to reach the apples at the top of the tree.

10   The supple gymnast was extremely _____ .

11   We receive our _____ through food.

12   The railway _____ was full of passengers.

13   We pulled into the _____ forecourt to fill the car with petrol.

14   The _____ height of my classmates is 140 cm.

15   I love to eat my _____ with cream and sugar on it.

16   Hermes was known as the _____ who served the Greek gods.

Ⓑ Which of your words have these smaller words hidden in them? [8]

1   car   _____

2   led   _____

3   pass   _____

4   edge   _____

5   ridge   _____

6   mess   _____

7   hall   _____

8   rage   _____

---

agile

average

carriage

challenge

energy

fridge

garage

general

generous

gently

ledge

marriage

messenger

passenger

porridge

sponge

24

💡 **Helpful Hint**

All of these words have a soft 'g' which makes it sound like a 'j'. Remember that when you sound out a word, a 'j' sound may be spelt with a 'g' or 'dg'.

Unit 3

berries

bodies

bunnies

daisies

elves

enemies

families

ladies

memories

mummies

noises

ourselves

replies

senses

soldiers

vegetables

30

Ⓒ Write the singlular form of the words in your list. [16]

1	elves	_____	9	enemies	_____
2	families	_____	10	ladies	_____
3	mummies	_____	11	memories	_____
4	vegetables	_____	12	bodies	_____
5	noises	_____	13	senses	_____
6	bunnies	_____	14	berries	_____
7	daisies	_____	15	soldiers	_____
8	replies	_____	16	ourselves	_____

Ⓓ Which of your words fit these definitions? [14]

1 The people we are related to   _____

2 Foods like carrots and sprouts   _____

3 People in the army   _____

4 Soft fruits   _____

5 Answers   _____

6 Rabbits   _____

7 Mothers   _____

8 Foes   _____

9 What we remember   _____

10 Sounds   _____

11 Sight, hearing, taste   _____

12 Flowers that grow on lawns   _____

13 Little fairy folk   _____

14 Women   _____

💡 **Helpful Hint**

When we pluralise a word ending in an 'f' we usually remove the 'f' and add 'ves'.
When we pluralise a word ending in a 'y', we usually remove the 'y' and add 'ies'.

E Fill in the grid with all of your words, using the clues to help you. [16]

Across

1   Person from Germany
3   Very cold
6   All together
8   Something with links
9   Person from Italy
13 Someone with no parents
14 A mark
15 Our bones

Down

1   To have become larger
2   A purpose
4   A point of view
5   Where the sky joins the land
7   Current style
10 To hear
11 A worry
12 A large house

F Which of your words have these smaller words hidden in them? [8]

1   own   _____   5   let   _____

2   man   _____   6   con   _____

3   ten   _____   7   pin   _____

4   pin   _____   8   ash   _____

G Although all of your words end in 'n', two words could have the 'n' removed and would still make a word. Write those two words below. [2]

1   _____   2   _____

chain

concern

fashion

frozen

German

grown

horizon

Italian

listen

mansion

opinion

orphan

reason

skeleton

stain

unison

26

album

develop

epic

intern

lawn

lisp

madam

medium

museum

problem

tomato

transform

uniform

unknown

volcano

wisdom

30

(H) Fill in the grid with all of your words. The first letter of each word has been given to help you. [16]

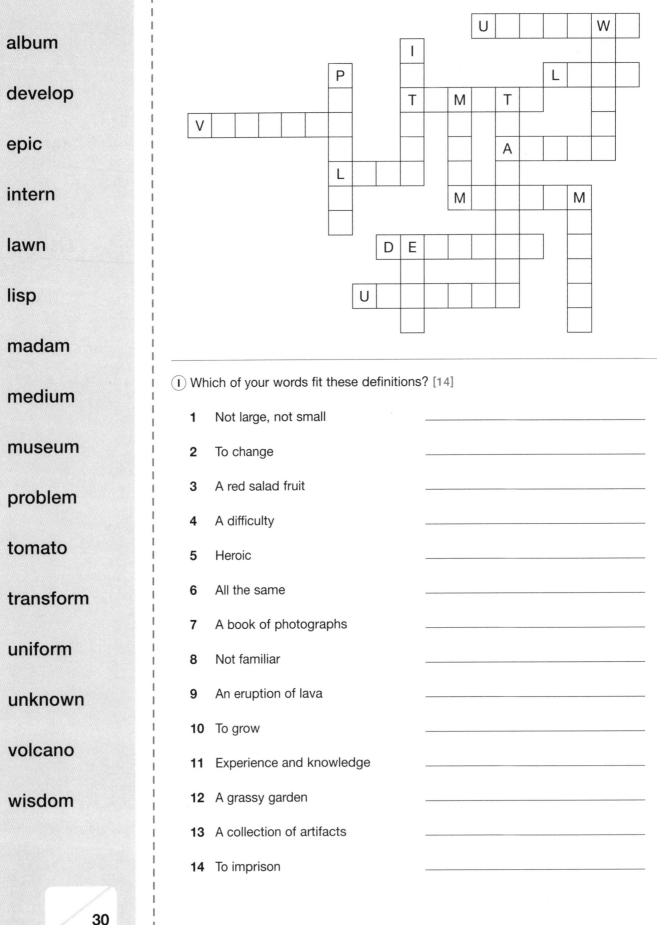

(I) Which of your words fit these definitions? [14]

1   Not large, not small _____

2   To change _____

3   A red salad fruit _____

4   A difficulty _____

5   Heroic _____

6   All the same _____

7   A book of photographs _____

8   Not familiar _____

9   An eruption of lava _____

10   To grow _____

11   Experience and knowledge _____

12   A grassy garden _____

13   A collection of artifacts _____

14   To imprison _____

(A) All of your words are hidden in the word search. They go across and down, but not diagonally. Find your words and then find the leftover letters. What do the leftover letters spell out? [17]

P	E	R	F	O	R	M	A	N	C	E
I	S	O	S	B	E	I	G	S	M	P
C	E	L	I	S	S	S	L	E	U	R
T	R	I	M	E	P	T	A	N	S	E
U	V	V	P	R	O	A	N	S	C	C
R	E	E	L	V	N	K	C	I	L	I
E	A	L	E	E	S	E	E	B	E	S
P	I	M	P	L	E	P	U	L	S	E
V	E	H	I	C	L	E	L	E	E	N
D	I	M	I	R	A	C	L	E	N	E

(B) Write the following words in the present participle form. Remember the spelling rule of removing 'e' before adding 'ing'. [6]

1 glance _glancing_

4 picture _____

2 mistake _____

5 pulse _____

3 observe _____

6 serve _____

(C) Which of your words are synonyms for these words? [12]

1 give out _____

7 easy _____

2 reply _____

8 imagine _____

3 error _____

9 wise _____

4 spot _____

10 show _____

5 exact _____

11 car or lorry _____

6 watch _____

12 throb _____

glance

miracle

mistake

muscle

observe

olive

performance

picture

pimple

precise

pulse

response

sensible

serve

simple

vehicle

35

Unit 4

according

chasing

coming

dancing

firing

flowing

hiding

hoping

listening

making

shining

slithering

staring

surprising

trying

wondering

32

D What is the root word of each of the following words? [16]

1	dancing	_____	9	chasing	_____
2	flowing	_____	10	hoping	_____
3	coming	_____	11	hiding	_____
4	listening	_____	12	according	_____
5	making	_____	13	firing	_____
6	shining	_____	14	slithering	_____
7	surprising	_____	15	wondering	_____
8	staring	_____	16	trying	_____

E Which of your words fit into the rhyme below so that it makes sense? [4]

1 Learning to skip was tricky, so the girl began crying.

But the teacher understood that the child was _____ .

2 The kindly, wise teacher was gentle and caring,

When she saw the other children were pointing and _____ .

3 She wanted to stop the little girl's panic from rising,

So the teacher did something that was really _____ .

4 She let the whole class choose either skipping or prancing,

And then praised the little girl on her beautiful _____ .

F Which of your words are synonyms for these words? [12]

1	attempting	_____	7	shooting	_____
2	wishing	_____	8	arriving	_____
3	gleaming	_____	9	waltzing	_____
4	hearing	_____	10	thinking	_____
5	creating	_____	11	astonishing	_____
6	pursuing	_____	12	masking	_____

💡 **Helpful Hint**

When we turn a root word that ends in 'e' into the present participle, we remove the 'e' before adding the suffix 'ing'.

G All of your words fit into the grid. Work out which number represents each letter to solve the puzzle. [21]

A	B	C	D	E	F	G	H	I	K	L	M	N	O	P	R	S	T	U	V	W	Y
				22																	

H All of these words have at least one 's' at the beginning or end. Find the seven words that make another word when we remove an 's'. [7]

1 _____ 5 _____

2 _____ 6 _____

3 _____ 7 _____

4 _____

I Which of your words have these smaller words hidden in them? [6]

1 warm _____ 4 stand _____

2 stem _____ 5 hive _____

3 way _____ 6 had _____

Word list:

always

figures

sandals

sausage

scorch

shadow

shivered

spare

spirits

stalk

standard

starve

stumble

survive

swarmed

system

34

Unit 4

ability

activity

category

charity

discovery

empty

envy

finally

journey

nursery

pansy

parsley

penalty

storey

study

surely

28

(J) Fill in the grid with all of your words. The first letter of each word has been given to help you. [16]

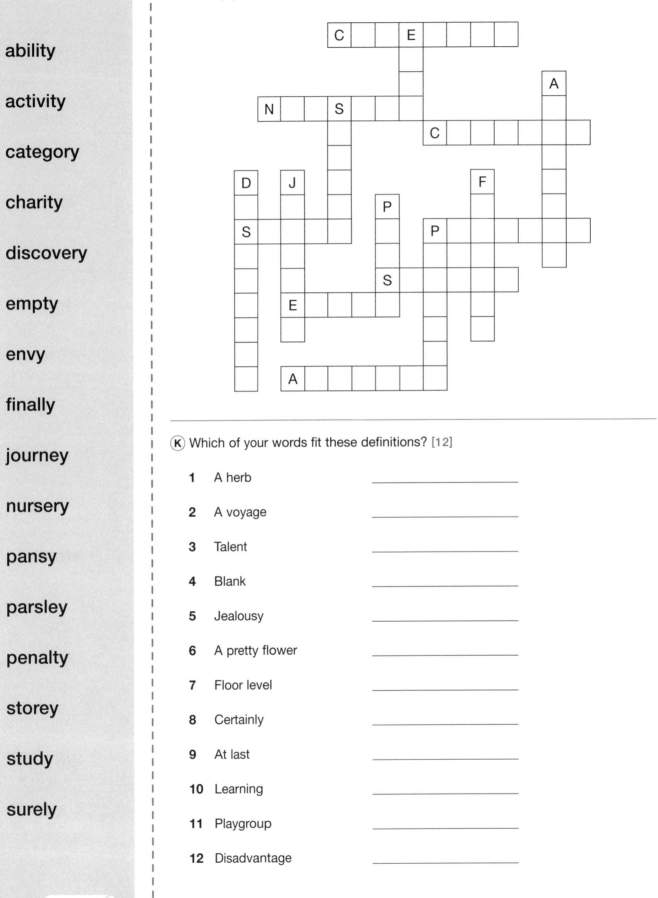

(K) Which of your words fit these definitions? [12]

1   A herb _____

2   A voyage _____

3   Talent _____

4   Blank _____

5   Jealousy _____

6   A pretty flower _____

7   Floor level _____

8   Certainly _____

9   At last _____

10   Learning _____

11   Playgroup _____

12   Disadvantage _____

 Recap

Ⓐ Draw line to match each word to its definition. [16]

1	major	A large animal
2	amateur	A bed cover
3	muscular	Compartment in clothes for carrying things
4	scar	A writer
5	author	A problem
6	burglar	Really important
7	emperor	Not an expert
8	instructor	To draw attention to something
9	elegant	Having big muscles
10	elephant	Insisting that you follow the rules
11	servant	The mark of an old injury
12	strict	Someone who serves
13	pocket	Someone who steals from a building
14	blanket	A coach or teacher
15	highlight	A ruler of an empire
16	fault	Smart or sophisticated

Ⓑ Which of your words have these smaller words hidden in them? [8]

1	leg	_____	**5**	lank	_____
2	per	_____	**6**	tor	_____
3	car	_____	**7**	mat	_____
4	van	_____	**8**	light	_____

Ⓒ Two of your words are made up of two shorter words. Write them below. [2]

1 _____ + _____ = _____

2 _____ + _____ = _____

amateur

author

blanket

burglar

elegant

elephant

emperor

fault

highlight

instructor

major

muscular

pocket

scar

servant

strict

26

Unit 5

boulder

cough

council

county

couple

crouch

disastrous

double

doubt

furious

mould

mound

mourn

rough

scout

shoulders

26

Ⓓ All of your words fit into the grid. Work out which number represents each letter to solve the puzzle. [18]

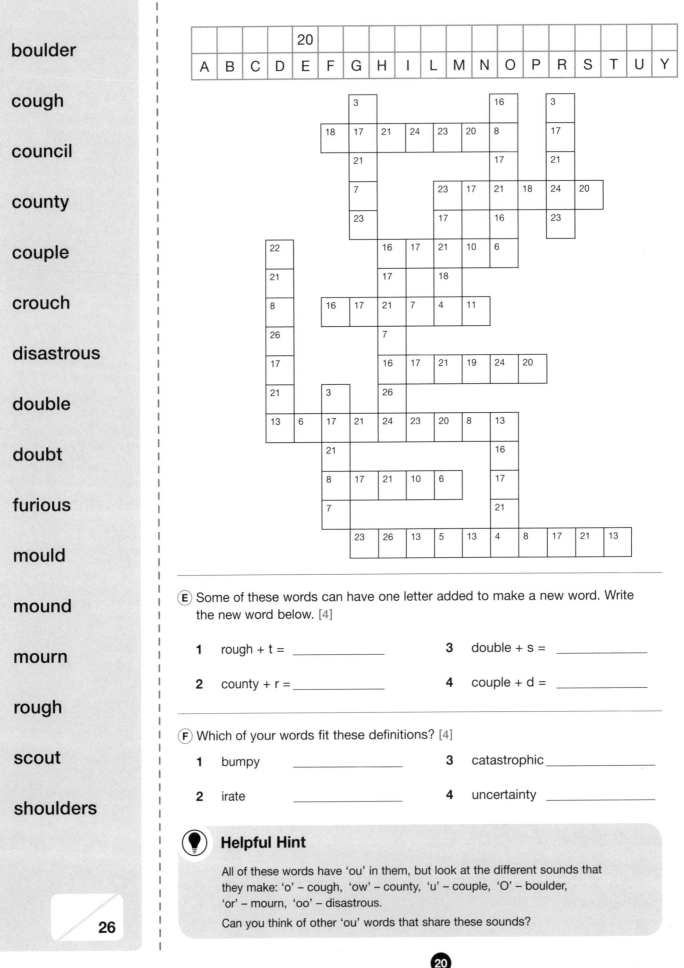

Ⓔ Some of these words can have one letter added to make a new word. Write the new word below. [4]

1 rough + t = _____

2 county + r = _____

3 double + s = _____

4 couple + d = _____

Ⓕ Which of your words fit these definitions? [4]

1 bumpy   _____

2 irate   _____

3 catastrophic _____

4 uncertainty _____

💡 **Helpful Hint**

All of these words have 'ou' in them, but look at the different sounds that they make: 'o' – cough, 'ow' – county, 'u' – couple, 'O' – boulder, 'or' – mourn, 'oo' – disastrous.

Can you think of other 'ou' words that share these sounds?

G All of the words in your list are made up of two shorter words. Join the pairs of words together. [16]

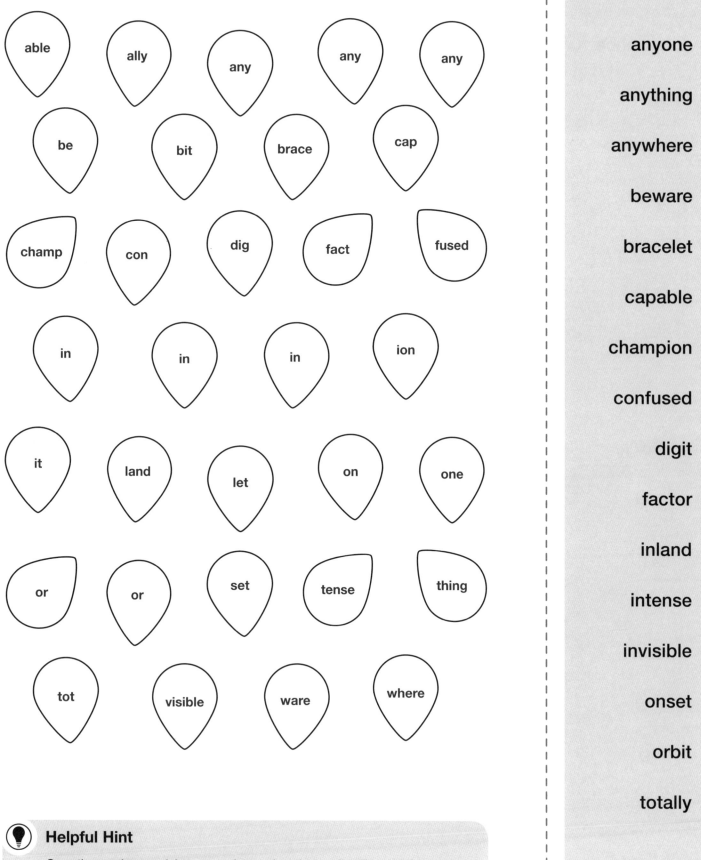

able	ally	any	any	any
be	bit	brace	cap	
champ	con	dig	fact	fused
in	in	in	ion	
it	land	let	on	one
or	or	set	tense	thing
tot	visible	ware	where	

anyone

anything

anywhere

beware

bracelet

capable

champion

confused

digit

factor

inland

intense

invisible

onset

orbit

totally

16

💡 **Helpful Hint**

Sometimes, when you join two words together, the words still sound the same.
Example: 'black' + 'bird' = blackbird.

Sometimes, however, the sound of the new word can be different.
Example: 'fat' + 'her' = father.

Unit 5

Bond SATs Skills Spelling and Vocabulary 10–11

conscience

debt

design

disguise

ghost

gnome

knocked

knot

scene

sighed

solemn

tomb

wrinkle

writing

wrong

yacht

34

(H) Underline the silent letters that we do not hear in these words. [16]

1 debt
2 disguise
3 ghost
4 knot
5 scene
6 sighed
7 wrinkle
8 wrong

9 design
10 gnome
11 knocked
12 solemn
13 conscience
14 tomb
15 writing
16 yacht

(I) Which of your words fit these definitions? [8]

1 A spectre _____

2 Serious _____

3 A boat _____

4 Breathed _____

5 Incorrect _____

6 Crease _____

7 Pattern _____

8 Using a pen _____

(J) Which of your words rhyme with the words below? [10]

1 room _____

2 foam _____

3 roast _____

4 mean _____

5 met _____

6 most _____

7 rot _____

8 tied _____

9 fighting _____

10 locked _____

Recap

22

Answers

Worked word searches can be found at the back of this book.

Unit 1

(A) 1 twirl – to twist or spin
2 bridal – to do with a wedding
3 plaits – braided hair or thread
4 blank – a missing space
5 grateful – appreciative
6 laundry – washing
7 powerful – strong
8 social – community or communal
9 wonderful – fantastic
10 selfish – not generous or thoughtful
11 claim – to make a statement
12 plastic – a material
13 uncle – my mother's or father's brother
14 style – fashion
15 temple – a place of worship
16 lug – to drag, pull or heave

(B) 1 plastic　3 laundry　5 powerful　7 claim
2 grateful　4 bridal　6 selfish　8 blank

(C) 1 twirl　3 blank　5 powerful
2 wonderful　4 grateful　6 claim

(D)
24	15	3	11	8	21	22	10	4	14	5	17	12	18	23	25	7	13	20	2
A	B	C	D	E	F	G	H	I	L	N	O	P	R	S	T	U	V	W	Y

(E) **1-2 In any order:** ion, riot

(F) **1-4 In any order:** brilliant, grief, alien, nuisance

(G) 1 superior　　　　3 relief
2 grief　　　　　　4 alien

(H) **Across:**　　　　**Down:**
2 query　　　　　　1 cruel
4 queue　　　　　　3 bruise
7 liquid　　　　　　5 equator
8 glue　　　　　　　6 square
11 fuel　　　　　　　9 valuable
12 squirrel　　　　　10 achieves
14 biscuits　　　　　11 fluid
15 avenue　　　　　13 rescue

(I) 1 achieving　3 bruising　5 querying
2 rescuing　4 squirrelling　6 queuing

(J) 1 alter　　　　　9 hover
2 quiver　　　　　10 partner
3 corner　　　　　11 customer
4 crater　　　　　12 together
5 danger　　　　　13 splinter
6 number　　　　14 helicopter
7 prefer　　　　　15 register
8 lobster　　　　　16 disaster

(K) 1 danger　　4 prefer　　7 together
2 splinter　5 alter　　8 quiver
3 customer　6 disaster

(L) 1 falter　　　　2 customers

(M) 1 over　　　　　3 cater
2 anger　　　　　4 refer

Unit 2

(A) **Leftover letters spell:** END WITH 'TION'

(B) 1 converse　　　　7 operate
2 decorate　　　　8 protect
3 describe　　　　9 attend
4 direct　　　　　10 attract
5 invent　　　　　11 inform
6 complete　　　　12 instruct

(C)
```
              S
              T
  C O V E R E D    T O R T
  P         M U      T
  E   B     R P R O D U C E D
F R O W N E D   D     R   E
I   T     I T       E   E W
N   H   R E T U R N E D   A
L I N E D   N   C       N
S   H     E N   D O D G E D
H   E     N C       R E
E   D     T U S       E D
D         E           D
    H A U N T E D
          E
C L I M B E D
```

(D) 1 frowned　　　　9 bothered
2 climbed　　　　10 returned
3 wandered　　　11 dodged
4 bothered　　　12 encrusted
5 finished　　　　13 tortured
6 striped　　　　14 produced
7 returned　　　15 haunted
8 covered　　　　16 frowned

(E)
11	1	18	4	20	3	21	7	10	17	15	26	14	19	6	13	24	22	5	2
A	B	C	D	E	G	I	J	K	L	M	N	O	P	R	S	T	U	V	X

(F) 1 telescope　　　7 exaggerate
2 pause　　　　　8 voice
3 trickle　　　　　9 joke
4 relative　　　　10 accommodate
5 visible　　　　　11 repulsive
6 curve　　　　　12 volume

(G) **Leftover letters spell:** THE END LETTER 'D'

(H) 1 wondered　　　8 overjoyed
2 hind　　　　　　9 timid
3 wand　　　　　10 poked
4 arid　　　　　　11 hatred
5 almond　　　　12 descend
6 answered　　　13 reward
7 crowd　　　　　14 record

Unit 3

(A) 1 gently　　　　9 challenge
2 marriage　　　10 agile
3 passenger　　11 energy
4 sponge　　　　12 carriage
5 generous　　　13 garage
6 fridge　　　　14 average
7 ledge　　　　15 porridge
8 general　　　16 messenger

(B) 1 carriage　　　5 fridge/porridge
2 ledge　　　　　6 messenger
3 passenger　　7 challenge
4 ledge　　　　　8 average/garage

(C) 1 elf　　　　　　9 enemy
2 family　　　　10 lady
3 mummy　　　　11 memory
4 vegetable　　12 body
5 noise　　　　　13 sense
6 bunny　　　　14 berry
7 daisy　　　　　15 soldier
8 reply　　　　　16 ourself

(D) 1 families / mummies　8 enemies
2 vegetables　　　　　9 memories
3 soldiers　　　　　　10 noises
4 berries　　　　　　11 senses
5 replies　　　　　　12 daisies
6 bunnies　　　　　　13 elves
7 mummies　　　　　14 ladies

(E) **Across:**
1 German
3 frozen
6 unison
8 chain
9 Italian
13 orphan
14 stain
15 skeleton

Down:
1 grown
2 reason
4 opinion
5 horizon
7 fashion
10 listen
11 concern
12 mansion

(F)
1 grown
2 German/mansion
3 listen
4 opinion
5 skeleton
6 concern
7 opinion
8 fashion

(G) **1-2 In any order:** grown, frozen

(H)
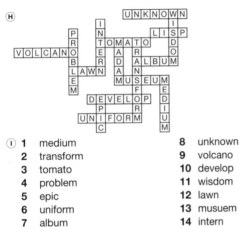

(I)
1 medium
2 transform
3 tomato
4 problem
5 epic
6 uniform
7 album
8 unknown
9 volcano
10 develop
11 wisdom
12 lawn
13 musuem
14 intern

Unit 4

(A) **Leftover letters spell:** ALL END IN 'E'

(B)
1 glancing
2 mistaking
3 observing
4 picturing
5 pulsing
6 serving

(C)
1 serve
2 response
3 mistake
4 pimple
5 precise
6 observe
7 simple
8 picture
9 sensible
10 performance
11 vehicle
12 pulse

(D)
1 dance
2 flow
3 come
4 listen
5 make
6 shine
7 surprise
8 stare
9 chase
10 hope
11 hide
12 accord
13 fire
14 slither
15 wonder
16 try

(E)
1 trying
2 staring
3 surprising
4 dancing

(F)
1 trying
2 hoping
3 shining
4 listening
5 making
6 chasing
7 firing
8 coming
9 dancing
10 wondering
11 surprising
12 hiding

(G)

24	10	14	4	22	13	23	18	8	5	9	19	25	17	1	3	7	21	11	2	15	16
A	B	C	D	E	F	G	H	I	K	L	M	N	O	P	R	S	T	U	V	W	Y

(H) **1-7 In any order:** swarmed (warmed), sandals (sandal), spirits (spirit), spare (pare), figures (figure), stalk (talk), stumble (tumble)

(I)
1 swarmed
2 system
3 always
4 standard
5 shivered
6 shadow

(J)
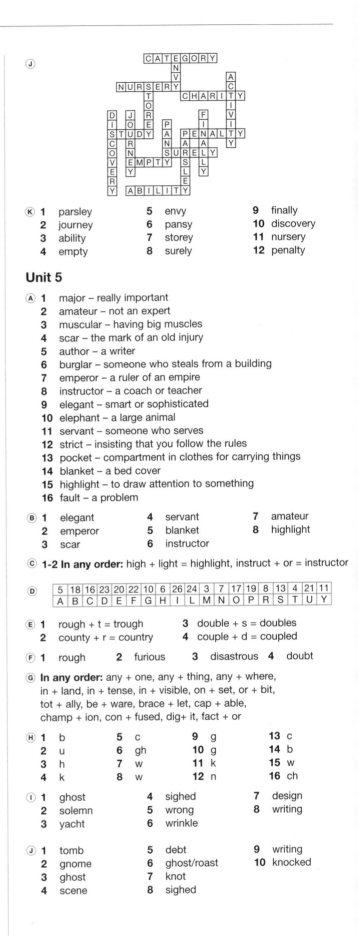

(K)
1 parsley
2 journey
3 ability
4 empty
5 envy
6 pansy
7 storey
8 surely
9 finally
10 discovery
11 nursery
12 penalty

Unit 5

(A)
1 major – really important
2 amateur – not an expert
3 muscular – having big muscles
4 scar – the mark of an old injury
5 author – a writer
6 burglar – someone who steals from a building
7 emperor – a ruler of an empire
8 instructor – a coach or teacher
9 elegant – smart or sophisticated
10 elephant – a large animal
11 servant – someone who serves
12 strict – insisting that you follow the rules
13 pocket – compartment in clothes for carrying things
14 blanket – a bed cover
15 highlight – to draw attention to something
16 fault – a problem

(B)
1 elegant
2 emperor
3 scar
4 servant
5 blanket
6 instructor
7 amateur
8 highlight

(C) **1-2 In any order:** high + light = highlight, instruct + or = instructor

(D)

5	18	16	23	20	22	10	6	26	24	3	7	17	19	8	13	4	21	11
A	B	C	D	E	F	G	H	I	L	M	N	O	P	R	S	T	U	Y

(E)
1 rough + t = trough
2 county + r = country
3 double + s = doubles
4 couple + d = coupled

(F)
1 rough
2 furious
3 disastrous
4 doubt

(G) **In any order:** any + one, any + thing, any + where, in + land, in + tense, in + visible, on + set, or + bit, tot + ally, be + ware, brace + let, cap + able, champ + ion, con + fused, dig+ it, fact + or

(H)
1 b
2 u
3 h
4 k
5 c
6 gh
7 w
8 w
9 g
10 g
11 k
12 n
13 c
14 b
15 w
16 ch

(I)
1 ghost
2 solemn
3 yacht
4 sighed
5 wrong
6 wrinkle
7 design
8 writing

(J)
1 tomb
2 gnome
3 ghost
4 scene
5 debt
6 ghost/roast
7 knot
8 sighed
9 writing
10 knocked

Unit 6

(A)

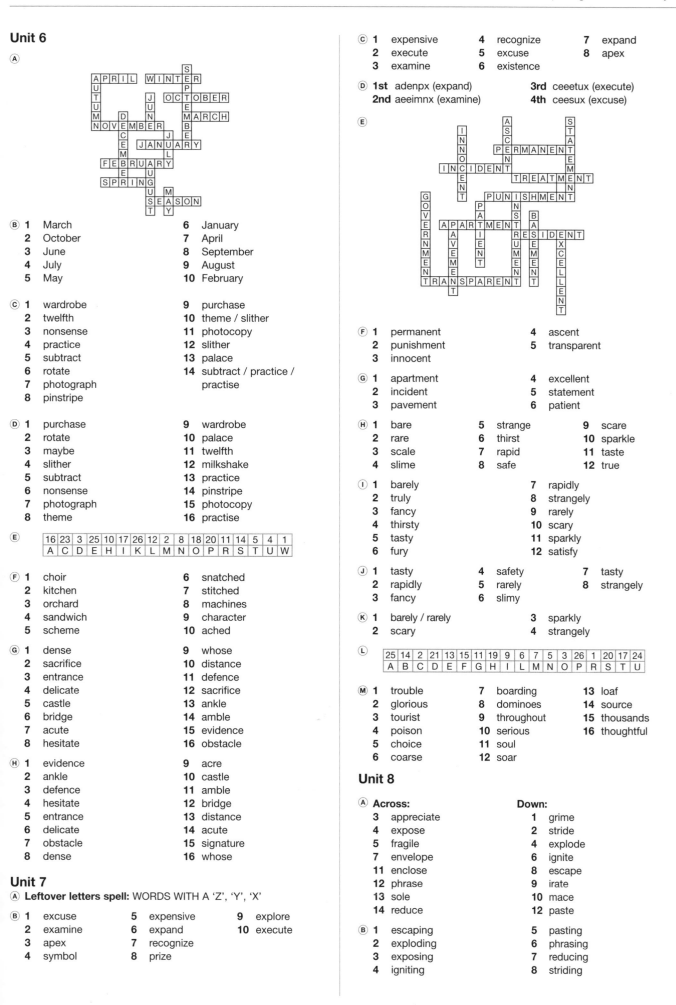

(B)
1	March	6	January
2	October	7	April
3	June	8	September
4	July	9	August
5	May	10	February

(C)
1	wardrobe	9	purchase
2	twelfth	10	theme / slither
3	nonsense	11	photocopy
4	practice	12	slither
5	subtract	13	palace
6	rotate	14	subtract / practice /
7	photograph		practise
8	pinstripe		

(D)
1	purchase	9	wardrobe
2	rotate	10	palace
3	maybe	11	twelfth
4	slither	12	milkshake
5	subtract	13	practice
6	nonsense	14	pinstripe
7	photograph	15	photocopy
8	theme	16	practise

(E)
16	23	3	25	10	17	26	12	2	8	18	20	11	14	5	4	1
A	C	D	E	H	I	K	L	M	N	O	P	R	S	T	U	W

(F)
1	choir	6	snatched
2	kitchen	7	stitched
3	orchard	8	machines
4	sandwich	9	character
5	scheme	10	ached

(G)
1	dense	9	whose
2	sacrifice	10	distance
3	entrance	11	defence
4	delicate	12	sacrifice
5	castle	13	ankle
6	bridge	14	amble
7	acute	15	evidence
8	hesitate	16	obstacle

(H)
1	evidence	9	acre
2	ankle	10	castle
3	defence	11	amble
4	hesitate	12	bridge
5	entrance	13	distance
6	delicate	14	acute
7	obstacle	15	signature
8	dense	16	whose

Unit 7

(A) **Leftover letters spell:** WORDS WITH A 'Z', 'Y', 'X'

(B)
1	excuse	5	expensive	9	explore
2	examine	6	expand	10	execute
3	apex	7	recognize		
4	symbol	8	prize		

(C)
1	expensive	4	recognize	7	expand
2	execute	5	excuse	8	apex
3	examine	6	existence		

(D)
1st	adenpx (expand)	**3rd**	ceeetux (execute)
2nd	aeeimnx (examine)	**4th**	ceesux (excuse)

(E)

(F)
1	permanent	4	ascent
2	punishment	5	transparent
3	innocent		

(G)
1	apartment	4	excellent
2	incident	5	statement
3	pavement	6	patient

(H)
1	bare	5	strange	9	scare
2	rare	6	thirst	10	sparkle
3	scale	7	rapid	11	taste
4	slime	8	safe	12	true

(I)
1	barely	7	rapidly
2	truly	8	strangely
3	fancy	9	rarely
4	thirsty	10	scary
5	tasty	11	sparkly
6	fury	12	satisfy

(J)
1	tasty	4	safety	7	tasty
2	rapidly	5	rarely	8	strangely
3	fancy	6	slimy		

(K)
1	barely / rarely	3	sparkly
2	scary	4	strangely

(L)
25	14	2	21	13	15	11	19	9	6	7	5	3	26	1	20	17	24
A	B	C	D	E	F	G	H	I	L	M	N	O	P	R	S	T	U

(M)
1	trouble	7	boarding	13	loaf
2	glorious	8	dominoes	14	source
3	tourist	9	throughout	15	thousands
4	poison	10	serious	16	thoughtful
5	choice	11	soul		
6	coarse	12	soar		

Unit 8

(A) **Across:**
3	appreciate
4	expose
5	fragile
7	envelope
11	enclose
12	phrase
13	sole
14	reduce

Down:
1	grime
2	stride
4	explode
6	ignite
8	escape
9	irate
10	mace
12	paste

(B)
1	escaping	5	pasting
2	exploding	6	phrasing
3	exposing	7	reducing
4	igniting	8	striding

(C) **Leftover letters spell:** THEY END IN 'Y'

(D)
1	Thursday	7	literacy
2	Saturday	8	mystery
3	Sunday	9	money
4	delivery	10	destroy
5	Friday	11	holiday
6	heavy	12	military

(E)

(F)
1	petrol	5	initial	9	awful
2	spiteful	6	label	10	dismal
3	parcel	7	several	11	control
4	personal	8	official	12	original

(G)
1	nation	4	remove
2	origin	5	spite
3	person		

(H)
1	awful	3	national	5	control
2	initial	4	removal	6	spiteful

(I)
25	26	14	12	23	19	18	8	22	13	20	21	16	7	15	1	10	11	9
A	C	D	E	F	G	I	K	L	M	N	O	R	S	T	U	V	X	Y

(J)
1	nosy	2	exactly	3	lively	4	luckily

(K)
1	angry	3	exact	5	guilt	7	lucky
2	cost	4	excite	6	love	8	nose

Unit 9

(A)
1	dripping	9	worrying
2	hurriedly	10	torrent
3	umbrella	11	chopped
4	surrender	12	arrival
5	blurred	13	terrible / horrible
6	dropped	14	arrange
7	horrible / terrible	15	starry
8	mirror	16	communicate

(B)
1	worry	3	hurry	5	drip	7	chop
2	blur	4	drop	6	arrive	8	star

(C) **Across:**
1	lilac
4	departure
8	iceberg
10	camera
12	picnic
13	harsh
14	balance
15	criminal
16	rigid

Down:
2	altar
3	victim
5	paragraph
6	foreign
7	arena
9	spectacle
11	earlier

(D)
1	rigid	6	camera	11	criminal
2	harsh	7	arena	12	balance
3	victim	8	picnic	13	foreign
4	lilac	9	earlier	14	departure
5	altar	10	paragraph		

(E)
1	I burst	6	I seek	11	I slide
2	I cling	7	I stick	12	I sweep
3	I sleep	8	I bury	13	I deal
4	I spin	9	I creep	14	I spy
5	I dream	10	I fling	15	I strike

(F)
1	struck	5	spun	9	burst
2	sought	6	slid	10	flung
3	stuck	7	kept		
4	swept	8	buried		

(G)
1	lung	4	lid	7	pun
2	deal	5	ought	8	truck
3	dream	6	wept	9	tuck

(H) **Leftover letters spell:** THERE'S A SOFT 'C' IN ALL THE WORDS

(I)
1	circular	5	cancel	9	except
2	fierce	6	excited	10	silence
3	novice	7	ascend		
4	centimetres	8	central		

Unit 10

(A)
18	26	22	13	12	3	19	6	8	10	15	9	25	24	21	1	23	11	4	7	2
A	C	D	E	G	H	I	K	L	M	N	O	P	Q	R	S	T	U	V	W	Y

(B)
1	crease	3	creative	5	please
2	plead	4	leather	6	creature

(C)
1	create	2	search	3	lead	4	creak

(D)
1	exist	5	robot	9	malt	13	secret
2	reflect	6	concert	10	abduct	14	perfect
3	urgent	7	pelt	11	trust	15	result
4	relevant	8	neglect	12	market	16	portrait

(E)
1	urgent	5	perfect	9	abduct	13	secret
2	result	6	concert	10	neglect	14	robot
3	market	7	trust	11	exist		
4	portrait	8	reflect	12	malt		

(F)
1	exit	3	pet	5	root
2	mat	4	rust		

(G) **Across:**
1	allowed
3	blossom
5	assume
7	stunned
9	assure
10	willow
12	traveller
13	bullying

Down:
1	assist
2	assent
3	beginning
4	tunnel
6	jewellery
8	swollen
11	ballet
14	occupy

(H)
1	willow	5	ballet	9	assure
2	traveller	6	assume	10	beginning
3	jewellery	7	allowed		
4	blossom	8	assist		

(I)
1	cannot	2	assure	3	assist	4	allowed

(J)

(K)
1	batter	3	stab	5	chat	7	forget
2	drag	4	mass	6	snap	8	scribe

(L)
1	immense	7	programme
2	luggage	8	litter
3	forgotten	9	snapped
4	attic	10	pattern
5	scribble	11	dragged
6	chatting	12	recommend

(A) Fill in the grid with all of your words. The first letter of each word has been given to help you. [16]

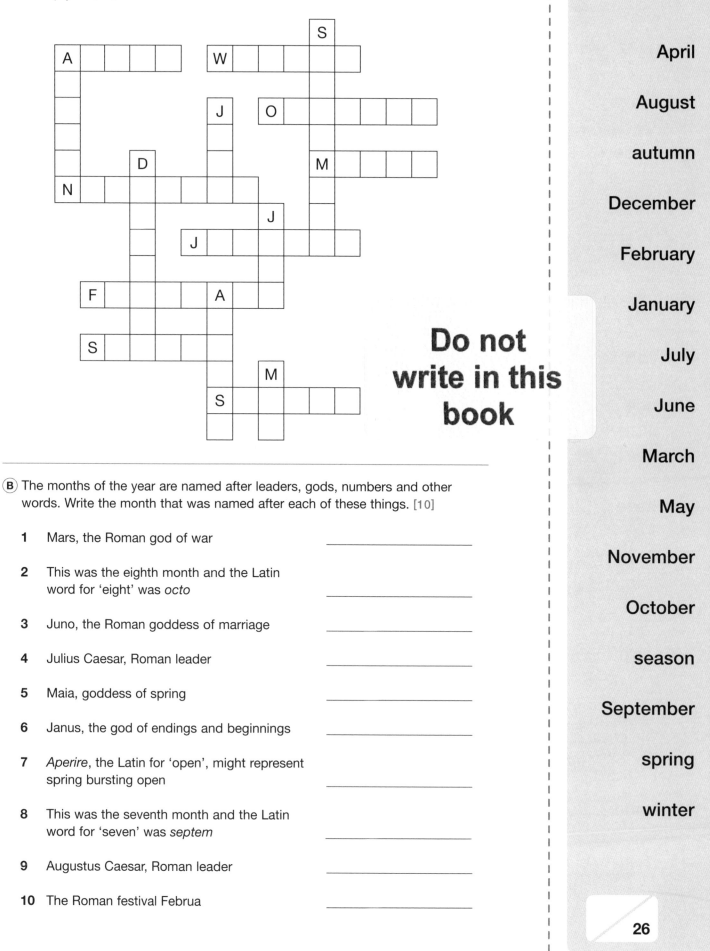

April

August

autumn

December

February

January

July

June

March

May

November

October

season

September

spring

winter

Do not write in this book

(B) The months of the year are named after leaders, gods, numbers and other words. Write the month that was named after each of these things. [10]

1   Mars, the Roman god of war   _____

2   This was the eighth month and the Latin
     word for 'eight' was *octo*   _____

3   Juno, the Roman goddess of marriage   _____

4   Julius Caesar, Roman leader   _____

5   Maia, goddess of spring   _____

6   Janus, the god of endings and beginnings   _____

7   *Aperire*, the Latin for 'open', might represent
     spring bursting open   _____

8   This was the seventh month and the Latin
     word for 'seven' was *septem*   _____

9   Augustus Caesar, Roman leader   _____

10   The Roman festival Februa   _____

26

Unit 6

maybe

milkshake

nonsense

palace

photocopy

photograph

pinstripe

practice

practise

purchase

rotate

slither

subtract

theme

twelfth

wardrobe

30

Ⓒ Which of your words have these smaller words hidden in them? You may need to use some of your words more than once. [14]

1	rob	_____	8	rip	_____
2	elf	_____	9	has	_____
3	on	_____	10	the	_____
4	ice	_____	11	cop	_____
5	sub	_____	12	lit	_____
6	ate	_____	13	ace	_____
7	tog	_____	14	act	_____

Ⓓ Which of your words fit these definitions? [16]

1   To buy   _____

2   To turn   _____

3   Possibly   _____

4   Slide   _____

5   To take away   _____

6   Rubbish   _____

7   A camera picture   _____

8   Topic   _____

9   A clothes cupboard   _____

10 A royal home   _____

11 After 'eleventh'   _____

12 A dairy drink   _____

13 A place for a doctor or dentist   _____

14 A fabric with a thin stripe   _____

15 To print a duplicate   _____

16 To rehearse   _____

💡 **Helpful Hint**

A quick way of remembering when to use practice ('c') and practise ('s') is that the noun uses 'c' while the verb uses 's' (for spellings) so I PRACTISE my SPELLINGS.

(E) All of your words fit into the grid. Work out which number represents each letter to solve the puzzle. [16]

											14		
A	C	D	E	H	I	K	L	M	N	O	P	R	S	T	U	W

20

17

23	10	16	11	16	23	5	25	11		5
10										23	10	18	17	11
18	11	23	10	16	11	3		12		10
23		10					16	23	10	25	3		14		14
18		18		14			4			3			16		23
12		26	17	5	23	10	25	8					8		10
16		25		18			23	10	4	23	26	25	3		25
5		3		2			10						1		2
25				16				2	16	23	10	17	8	25	14
14	8	16	5	23	10	25	3						23
		10				14	5	17	5	23	10	25	3

(F) Which of your words fit these definitions? [10]

1 A group of singers _____

2 A room we cook in _____

3 A group of fruit trees _____

4 A bread snack _____

5 A plot or plan _____

6 Stolen _____

7 Sewn _____

8 Electrical devices _____

9 Personality _____

10 Felt soreness _____

ached

character

chocolates

choir

choked

chucked

kitchen

launch

machines

orchard

pitched

sandwich

scheme

snatched

stitched

stomach

26

Unit 6

acute

amble

ankle

bridge

castle

defence

delicate

dense

distance

entrance

evidence

hesitate

obstacle

sacrifice

signature

whose

32

(G) An anagram is a word that has had its letters rearranged. Which of your words have become the following anagrams? [16]

1	sende	_____	9	sheow	_____
2	aircsecfi	_____	10	dancesit	_____
3	catneren	_____	11	feedcen	_____
4	lacetide	_____	12	geutranis	_____
5	lacest	_____	13	klean	_____
6	grideb	_____	14	blame	_____
7	caute	_____	15	diveceen	_____
8	asheetti	_____	16	lobescat	_____

(H) Which of your words fit these definitions? [16]

1   Proof   _____

2   Part of the leg   _____

3   Protection   _____

4   To falter   _____

5   Arrival   _____

6   Fragile   _____

7   Hurdle   _____

8   Thick, solid   _____

9   Give up a thing you value   _____

10   A fortified building   _____

11   A slow walk   _____

12   A road across water   _____

13   Length   _____

14   Sharp   _____

15   Your name written   _____

16   Belonging to   _____

Unit 7

(A) All of your words are hidden in the word search. They go across and down, but not diagonally. Find your words and then find the leftover letters. What do the leftover letters spell out? [17]

S	Y	M	B	O	L	P	R	I	Z	E
Y	E	X	P	E	N	S	I	V	E	X
O	X	E	X	P	L	O	R	E	W	I
K	A	X	E	X	E	C	U	T	E	S
E	M	P	X	O	Y	O	G	A	R	T
Y	I	A	C	J	A	Z	Z	P	D	E
O	N	N	U	S	W	W	I	E	T	N
L	E	D	S	H	N	A	Z	X	Y	C
K	X	R	E	C	O	G	N	I	Z	E

(B) Which of your words are synonyms for these words? [8]

1 reason _____   5 dear _____

2 inspect _____   6 increase _____

3 top _____   7 identify _____

4 sign _____   8 award _____

(C) Which of your words have these smaller words hidden in them? [8]

1 pen _____   5 use _____

2 cut _____   6 ten _____

3 exam _____   7 and _____

4 cog _____   8 ape _____

(D) Put all the letters in each word in alphabetical order. Then put the new words in alphabetical order. [4]

examine	excuse	execute	expand

_____   _____   _____   _____

1 _____   2 _____   3 _____   4 _____

apex

examine

excuse

execute

existence

expand

expensive

explore

jazz

prize

recognize

symbol

yawn

yoga

yoke

yolk

37

31

Unit 7

apartment

ascent

basement

excellent

government

incident

innocent

instrument

patient

pavement

permanent

punishment

resident

statement

transparent

treatment

27

(E) Fill in the grid with all of your words. The first letter of each word has been given to help you. [16]

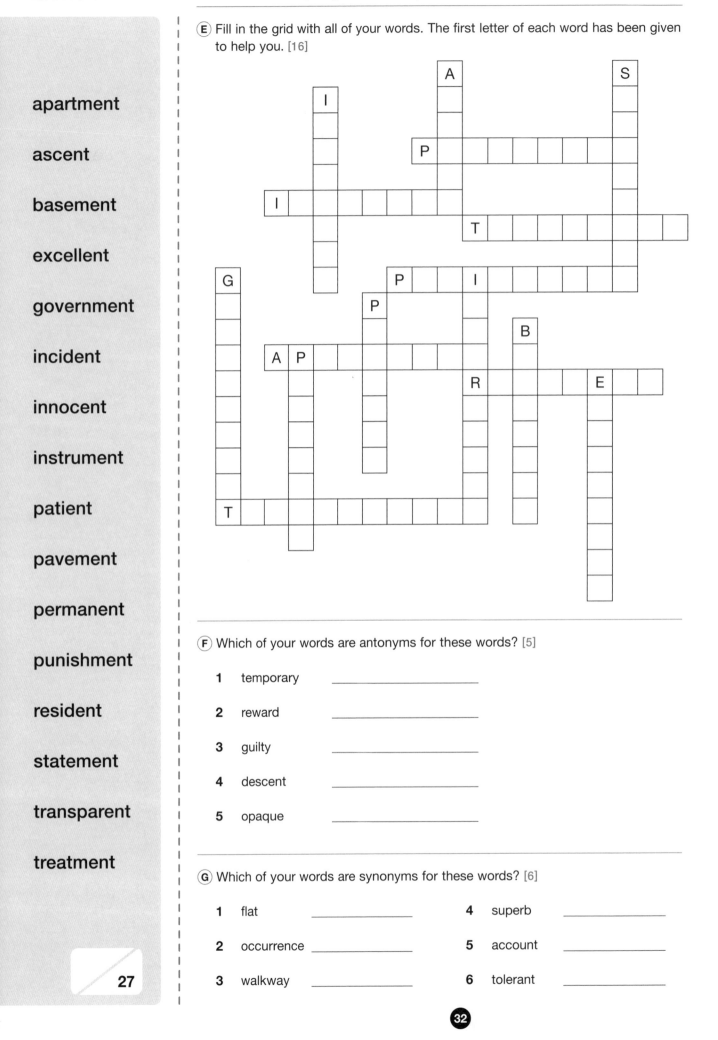

(F) Which of your words are antonyms for these words? [5]

1   temporary   _____

2   reward   _____

3   guilty   _____

4   descent   _____

5   opaque   _____

(G) Which of your words are synonyms for these words? [6]

1   flat   _____   4   superb   _____

2   occurrence   _____   5   account   _____

3   walkway   _____   6   tolerant   _____

(H) What is the root word of each of the following words? [12]

1	barely _____	**7**	rapidly _____
2	rarely _____	**8**	safety _____
3	scaly _____	**9**	scary _____
4	slimy _____	**10**	sparkly _____
5	strangely _____	**11**	tasty _____
6	thirsty _____	**12**	truly _____

(I) Which of your words are synonyms for these words? [12]

1	hardly _____	**7**	quickly _____
2	honestly _____	**8**	weirdly _____
3	decorative _____	**9**	infrequently _____
4	parched _____	**10**	frightening _____
5	delicious _____	**11**	glittery _____
6	anger _____	**12**	reassure _____

(J) Which of your words are antonyms for these words? [8]

1	unpalatable _____	**5**	frequently _____
2	slowly _____	**6**	dry _____
3	plain _____	**7**	disgusting _____
4	danger _____	**8**	normally _____

(K) Which of your words have these smaller words hidden in them? [4]

1	are _____	**3**	park _____
2	car _____	**4**	range _____

barely

fancy

fury

rapidly

rarely

safety

satisfy

scaly

scary

security

slimy

sparkly

strangely

tasty

thirsty

truly

36

💡 **Helpful Hint**

All of these words end in 'y'. Sometimes, when we add a 'y' to the end of a word, we remove the final 'e' first. **Example:** 'scale' becomes 'scaly' and 'scare' becomes 'scary'. Can you think of other words that follow the same spelling pattern?

Unit 7

boarding

choice

coarse

dominoes

glorious

loaf

poison

serious

soar

soul

source

thoughtful

thousands

throughout

tourist

trouble

Ⓛ All of your words fit into the grid. Work out which number represents each letter to solve the puzzle. [17]

															17	
A	B	C	D	E	F	G	H	I	L	M	N	O	P	R	S	T	U

Ⓜ Which of your words are synonyms for these words? [16]

1	problem	_____	**9**	everywhere	_____
2	wonderful	_____	**10**	solemn	_____
3	visitor	_____	**11**	spirit	_____
4	toxin	_____	**12**	fly high	_____
5	option	_____	**13**	bread	_____
6	rough	_____	**14**	origin	_____
7	getting on	_____	**15**	lots	_____
8	a game	_____	**16**	pensive	_____

Unit 8

A Fill in the grid with all of your words, using the clues to help you. [16]

Across

3 Enjoy
4 Uncover
5 Delicate
7 For transporting a letter
11 Surround
12 Idiom, expression
13 Part of the foot
14 Lessen

Down

1 Dirt
2 Step
4 Blow up
6 Set on fire
8 Flee
9 Angry
10 Weapon
12 Glue

B Turn the following words into the present participle. [8]

Example: enclose _enclosing_

1 escape _____

2 explode _____

3 expose _____

4 ignite _____

5 paste _____

6 phrase _____

7 reduce _____

8 stride _____

appreciate

enclose

envelope

escape

explode

expose

fragile

grime

ignite

irate

mace

paste

phrase

reduce

sole

stride

💡 **Helpful Hint**

Don't forget your spelling rules when adding the 'ing' suffix. Remove the 'e' before adding 'ing'.

24

Unit 8

already

delivery

destroy

Friday

heavy

holiday

literacy

military

Monday

money

mystery

Saturday

secretary

Sunday

Thursday

Tuesday

29

C All of your words are hidden in the word search. They go across and down, but not diagonally. Find your words and then find the leftover letters. What do the leftover letters spell out? [17]

L	T	M	S	U	N	D	A	Y	H	E	H	S
I	M	I	A	D	E	S	T	R	O	Y	O	E
T	O	L	T	H	U	R	S	D	A	Y	L	C
E	N	I	U	H	E	A	V	Y	Y	E	I	R
R	D	T	R	M	O	N	E	Y	N	D	D	E
A	A	A	D	E	L	I	V	E	R	Y	A	T
C	Y	R	A	L	R	E	A	D	Y	I	Y	A
Y	N	Y	Y	M	Y	S	T	E	R	Y	Y	R
F	R	I	D	A	Y	T	U	E	S	D	A	Y

D Which of your words fit these definitions? [12]

1 The day of the Norse god Thor _____

2 The day of the Roman god Saturn _____

3 The day of the sun _____

4 The dropping off of a parcel _____

5 The day of the Norse goddess Frigga _____

6 Weighty _____

7 Reading and writing _____

8 A conundrum or enigma _____

9 Finance _____

10 To ruin _____

11 Vacation _____

12 Army, navy, air force _____

(E) Fill in the grid with all of your words. The first letter of each word has been given to help you. [16]

(F) Which of your words are synonyms for these words? [12]

1	fuel	_____	7	many	_____
2	mean	_____	8	certified	_____
3	package	_____	9	dreadful	_____
4	individual	_____	10	dreary	_____
5	first	_____	11	supervise	_____
6	sticker	_____	12	authentic	_____

(G) What is the root word of each of the following words? [5]

1	national	_____	4	removal	_____
2	original	_____	5	spiteful	_____
3	personal	_____			

(H) Which of your words are antonyms for these words? [6]

1	wonderful	_____	4	addition	_____
2	final	_____	5	chaos	_____
3	local	_____	6	kind	_____

awful

control

decimal

dismal

hostel

initial

label

national

official

original

parcel

personal

petrol

removal

several

spiteful

39

Unit 8

angrily

costly

dingy

exactly

excitedly

floury

forty

guilty

lively

lonely

lovely

luckily

nasty

normally

nosy

rosy

30

(i) All of your words fit into the grid. Work out which number represents each letter to solve the puzzle. [18]

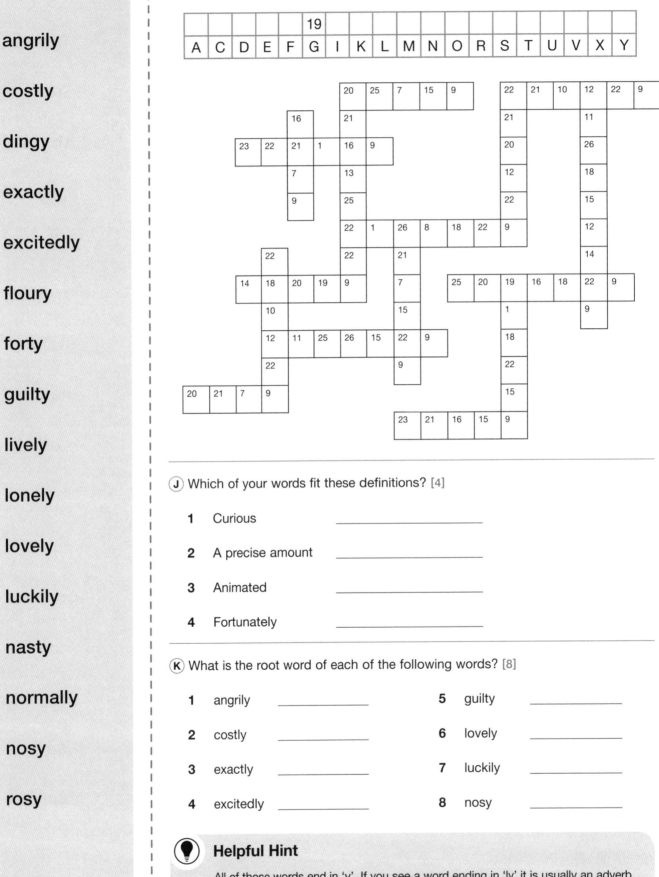

(j) Which of your words fit these definitions? [4]

1   Curious   _____

2   A precise amount   _____

3   Animated   _____

4   Fortunately   _____

(k) What is the root word of each of the following words? [8]

1   angrily   _____   5   guilty   _____

2   costly   _____   6   lovely   _____

3   exactly   _____   7   luckily   _____

4   excitedly _____   8   nosy   _____

💡 **Helpful Hint**

All of these words end in 'y'. If you see a word ending in 'ly' it is usually an adverb as it describes how something is done. **Example:** 'ran quickly'. Words ending in 'ly' can also be adjectives when they describe a noun. **Example:** 'costly mistake'.

A Place one of your words in each space so that the sentences make sense. [16]

1 We need a plumber to stop that tap from _____ .

2 We _____ raced to the bus stop, hoping not to be too late.

3 I need my _____ today as it is raining and I shall be outdoors.

4 The British commander had to _____ after he lost the battle.

5 After the optician put eye drops in, my eyesight was _____ .

6 He _____ the ball before running away.

7 Having toothache was _____ as I couldn't enjoy the party.

8 Grandma saw her new hairstyle in the _____ and smiled.

9 It was no good _____ about his exam results.

10 The little brook broke its bank as the _____ of water flooded the land.

11 My eyes watered as I _____ the onions.

12 The Queen's _____ at the palace was watched by the crowds.

13 It was _____ to hear of the homes that had been flooded.

14 Could we _____ to meet up next weekend?

15 The cold, _____ night sky was so clear and bright.

16 The police used their radios to _____ .

B What is the root word of each of the following words? [8]

1 worrying _____

2 blurred _____

3 hurriedly _____

4 dropped _____

5 dripping _____

6 arrival _____

7 chopped _____

8 starry _____

arrange

arrival

blurred

chopped

communicate

dripping

dropped

horrible

hurriedly

mirror

starry

surrender

terrible

torrent

umbrella

worrying

💡 **Helpful Hint**

All of these words have double letters in them. If a word has two syllables, it often has a double consonant. **Example:** 'arrange' or 'torrent'. If a word ends with a single consonant with a single vowel before it, the consonant is often doubled before we add a suffix. **Example:** 'drip' becomes 'dripping'.

24

altar

arena

balance

camera

criminal

departure

earlier

foreign

harsh

iceberg

lilac

paragraph

picnic

rigid

spectacle

victim

30

(c) Fill in the grid with all of your words, using the clues to help you. [16]

Across

1   A purple colour
4   Leaving
8   A huge block of ice
10 Used in photography
12 A meal outdoors
13 Cruel
14 To create equality
15 An offender
16 Inflexible

Down

2   A raised area in a church
3   A casualty
5   Way of grouping sentences into chunks
6   From another country
7   Stadium
9   A vision
11 Previously

(d) An anagram is a word that has had its letters rearranged. Which of your words have become the following anagrams? [14]

1   digir   _____

2   rashh   _____

3   cimvit   _____

4   calli   _____

5   larat   _____

6   racema   _____

7   neara   _____

8   nipicc   _____

9   earlire   _____

10 gapraphar   _____

11 nalirimc   _____

12 canelab   _____

13 reginfo   _____

14 tapurudee   _____

Unit 9

E All of the words in your list are in the past tense. Write them in the present tense using 'I' before each word. [15]

Example: kept ___I keep___

1	burst	_____	8	buried	_____
2	clung	_____	9	crept	_____
3	slept	_____	10	flung	_____
4	spun	_____	11	slid	_____
5	dreamt	_____	12	swept	_____
6	sought	_____	13	dealt	_____
7	stuck	_____	14	spied	_____
			15	struck	_____

F Which of your words are synonyms for these words? [10]

1	hit	_____	6	glided	_____
2	searched	_____	7	retained	_____
3	glued	_____	8	covered	_____
4	brushed	_____	9	exploded	_____
5	rotated	_____	10	threw	_____

G Remove one letter from the following words to make a new word. [9]

1	clung	_____	6	swept	_____
2	dealt	_____	7	spun	_____
3	dreamt	_____	8	struck	_____
4	slid	_____	9	stuck	_____
5	sought	_____			

 Helpful Hint

When you turn a word that ends in 'ied' from the past to present tense, remove the 'ied' before adding a 'y'. **Example:** 'carried' becomes 'carry' and 'married' becomes 'marry'.

Word list (Unit 9):

buried
burst
clung
crept
dealt
dreamt
flung
kept
slept
slid
sought
spied
spun
struck
stuck
swept

34

Unit 9

acid

ascend

cancel

centimetres

central

ceremony

circular

circus

cities

citizen

criticise

except

excited

fierce

novice

silence

27

(H) All of your words are hidden in the word search. They go across and down, but not diagonally. Find your words and then find the leftover letters. What do the leftover letters spell out? [17]

C	E	N	T	I	M	E	T	R	E	S	T	C
I	C	O	C	C	A	X	F	H	X	I	E	E
R	A	V	I	I	S	C	I	A	C	L	C	N
C	N	I	T	R	C	E	E	C	I	E	I	T
U	C	C	I	C	E	P	R	I	T	N	T	R
L	E	E	E	U	N	T	C	D	E	C	I	A
A	L	R	S	D	E	E	S	D	E	Z	L
R	C	E	R	E	M	O	N	Y	A	S	E	O
C	R	I	T	I	C	I	S	E	F	T	N	C
I	N	A	L	L	T	H	E	W	O	R	D	S

(I) Which of your words fit these definitions? [10]

1 In a round shape _____

2 Vicious _____

3 Beginner _____

4 Units of measurement _____

5 Abandon _____

6 Enthusiastic _____

7 Climb up _____

8 In the middle _____

9 Not including _____

10 No noise _____

 **Helpful Hint**

All of these words have a soft 'c' sound, so when you sound out a word and hear the 's' sound, bear in mind that it might be a 'c' creating it!

 Recap   42

(A) All of your words fit into the grid. Work out which number represents each letter to solve the puzzle. [20]

	26																			
A	C	D	E	G	H	I	K	L	M	N	O	P	Q	R	S	T	U	V	W	Y

Word list:

creaky

crease

creative

creature

dreary

earthquake

ease

leader

leather

meadow

people

plead

please

repeat

searching

spread

(B) Which of your words fit these definitions? [6]

1 Fold   _____

2 Beg   _____

3 Imaginative   _____

4 Cowhide   _____

5 Make happy   _____

6 Animal   _____

(C) What is the root word of each of the following words? [4]

1 creative   _____

2 searching   _____

3 leader   _____

4 creaky   _____

30

Unit 10

abduct

concert

exist

malt

market

neglect

pelt

perfect

portrait

reflect

relevant

result

robot

secret

trust

urgent

36

Ⓓ An anagram is a word that has had its letters rearranged. Which of your words have become the following anagrams? [16]

1	stixe	_____	**9**	lamt	_____
2	clefter	_____	**10**	badcut	_____
3	grunte	_____	**11**	strut	_____
4	lveretna	_____	**12**	tramek	_____
5	bootr	_____	**13**	recets	_____
6	cotcren	_____	**14**	feecptr	_____
7	lept	_____	**15**	lurest	_____
8	clenget	_____	**16**	partriot	_____

Ⓔ Which of your words fit these definitions? [15]

1 Very important _____

2 The final answer _____

3 Some outdoor shops _____

4 A picture of a person _____

5 Ideal _____

6 Performance _____

7 To have faith in _____

8 To mirror _____

9 To kidnap _____

10 Mistreat _____

11 To have life _____

12 Steeped grain _____

13 Confidential _____

14 An automated machine _____

15 To hurl something _____

Ⓕ Remove one letter from the following words to make a new word. [5]

1	exist	_____	**4**	trust	_____
2	malt	_____	**5**	robot	_____
3	pelt	_____			

G Fill in the grid with all of your words, using the clues to help you. [16]

Across

1 Permitted
3 Bloom
5 Suppose
7 Amazed
9 Guarantee
10 A type of tree
12 Someone who travels
13 Intimidating

Down

1 Help
2 Agree
3 Starting
4 Underground passage
6 Rings, necklace, earrings?
8 Enlarged
11 A dance
14 To keep busy

allowed

assent

assist

assume

assure

ballet

beginning

blossom

bullying

jewellery

occupy

stunned

swollen

traveller

tunnel

willow

H Which of your words have these smaller words hidden in them? [10]

1 will _____

2 rave _____

3 well _____

4 loss _____

5 let _____

6 sum _____

7 owe _____

8 is _____

9 sure _____

10 inn _____

I Which of your words are antonyms for these words? [4]

1 able _____

2 discourage _____

3 hinder _____

4 forbidden _____

30

45

Unit 10

attic

battered

chatting

dragged

forgotten

immense

litter

luggage

massive

otter

pattern

programme

recommend

scribble

snapped

stabbed

/36

(J) Fill in the grid with all of your words. The first letter of each word has been given to help you. [16]

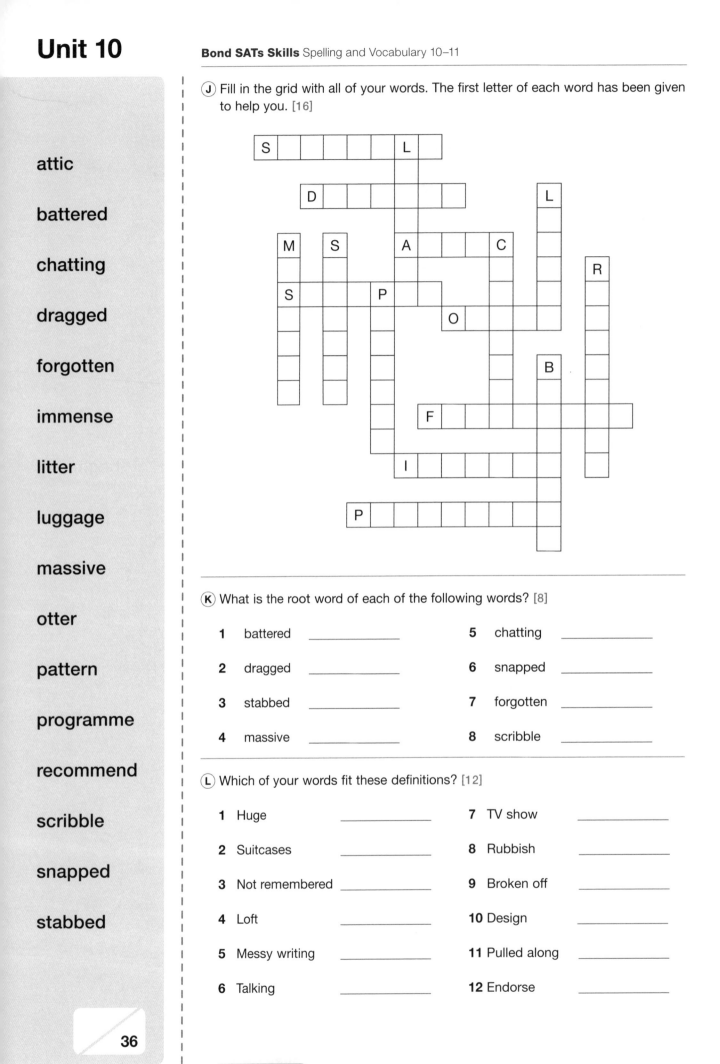

(K) What is the root word of each of the following words? [8]

1 battered _____

2 dragged _____

3 stabbed _____

4 massive _____

5 chatting _____

6 snapped _____

7 forgotten _____

8 scribble _____

(L) Which of your words fit these definitions? [12]

1 Huge _____

2 Suitcases _____

3 Not remembered _____

4 Loft _____

5 Messy writing _____

6 Talking _____

7 TV show _____

8 Rubbish _____

9 Broken off _____

10 Design _____

11 Pulled along _____

12 Endorse _____

Worked word searches

Unit 2

(A) **Leftover letters spell:** END WITH 'TION'

DESCRIPTIONS
EATTRACTIONE
CONVERSATION
OPROTECTIONS
RECEPTIONENA
ARDIRECTIONT
TATTENTIOND
TINVENTIONO
ONFORMATION
NOWCOMMOTION
INSTRUCTIONI
HTISECTIONON

(G) **Leftover letters spell:** THE END LETTER 'D'

DESCENDATOH
ARHINDHNVVE
REWARDASEH
CALENTWSRU
DONMPDREJM
LRDOOEERTO
TDTNKEDEEYT
WONDEREDDER
CROWDTIMIDD

Unit 4

(A) **Leftover letters spell:** ALL END IN 'E'

PERFORMANCE
SOSBEGSMP
CELSSSLEUR
TRMEPTANSE
UVVPROANSCC
REELVNKCLL
EALESEEBES
PIMPLEPULSE
VEHICLELEEN
DIMIRACLENE

Unit 7

(A) **Leftover letters spell:** WORDS WITH A 'Z', 'Y', 'X'

SYMBOLPRIZE
YEXPENSIVEX
OXEXPLOREWI
KAXEXECUTES
EMPXOYOGART
YIACJAZZPDE
ONNUSWWIETN
LEDSHNAZXYC
KXRECOGNIZE

Unit 8

(C) **Leftover letters spell:** THEY END IN 'Y'

LTMSUNDAYHEHS
MIADESTROYOE
TOLTHURSDAYLC
ENIUHEAVYYER
RDTRMONEYNDDE
AAADELIVERYAT
CYRALREADYIYA
YNYYMYSTERYYR
FRIDAYTUESDAY

Unit 9

(H) **Leftover letters spell:** THERE'S A SOFT 'C' IN ALL THE WORDS

CENTIMETRESTC
CCOCCAXFHXEE
RAVISCACLCN
CNITRCEECET
UCCICEPRINTR
LEEEUNTCDECA
ALRSSDEESDEZL
RCEREMONYASEO
CRITICISEFTNC
INALLTHEWORDS

Progress chart

How did you do? Fill in your score below and shade in the corresponding boxes to compare your progress across the different tests and units.

50%   100%

Unit 1, p3 Score: __ / 30

Unit 1, p4 Score: __ / 29

Unit 1, p5 Score: __ / 22

Unit 1, p6 Score: __ / 30

Unit 2, p7 Score: __ / 29

Unit 2, p8 Score: __ / 32

Unit 2, p9 Score: __ / 31

Unit 2, p10 Score: __ / 31

Unit 3, p11 Score: __ / 24

Unit 3, p12 Score: __ / 30

Unit 3, p13 Score: __ / 26

Unit 3, p14 Score: __ / 30

Unit 4, p15 Score: __ / 35

Unit 4, p16 Score: __ / 32

Unit 4, p17 Score: __ / 34

Unit 4, p18 Score: __ / 28

Unit 5, p19 Score: __ / 26

Unit 5, p20 Score: __ / 26

Unit 5, p21 Score: __ / 16

Unit 5, p22 Score: __ / 34

50%   100%

Unit 6, p27 Score: __ / 26

Unit 6, p28 Score: __ / 30

Unit 6, p29 Score: __ / 26

Unit 6, p30 Score: __ / 32

Unit 7, p31 Score: __ / 37

Unit 7, p32 Score: __ / 27

Unit 7, p33 Score: __ / 36

Unit 7, p34 Score: __ / 33

Unit 8, p35 Score: __ / 24

Unit 8, p36 Score: __ / 29

Unit 8, p37 Score: __ / 39

Unit 8, p38 Score: __ / 30

Unit 9, p39 Score: __ / 24

Unit 9, p40 Score: __ / 30

Unit 9, p41 Score: __ / 34

Unit 9, p42 Score: __ / 27

Unit 10, p43 Score: __ / 30

Unit 10, p44 Score: __ / 36

Unit 10, p45 Score: __ / 30

Unit 10, p46 Score: __ / 36